MAYA JADES

Bas relief carving on a flat Maya Jade showing a Maya dignitary seated on a throne. Late Classic period. This specimen was reported to have been found at Teotihuacan, but is in a similar style to jades from Nebaj.

MAYA JADES

ADRIAN DIGBY

PUBLISHED FOR
THE TRUSTEES OF THE BRITISH MUSEUM
BY
BRITISH MUSEUM PUBLICATIONS LIMITED

© 1972, The Trustees of the British Museum
First published 1964
Revised edition 1972
Reprinted 1978
ISBN 0 7141 1532 0 (*paper*)
ISBN 0 7141 1540 1 (*cased*)
Published by British Museum Publications Ltd
6 Bedford Square, London WC1B 3RA

The Department of Ethnography
is at 6 Burlington Gardens
LONDON W1X 2EX

Printed in Great Britain
at the University Press, Oxford
by Vivian Ridler
Printer to the University

CONTENTS

LIST OF ILLUSTRATIONS

PREFACE

Despite their great interest, little is known on the subject of Maya Jades. This may be due to the lack of precise information about them. Many famous pieces are casual finds without archaeological documentation, and the numerous specimens found under controlled conditions cannot be dated with any certainty or attributed to any particular locality, since they must often have been treasured for many generations before being buried in graves or votive caches.

The major source for the material discussed is the fine collection of Maya jades in the Ethnography Department of the British Museum. Other sources are the numerous excavation reports published by the division of historical research of the Carnegie Institution of Washington, and by the University Museum of Pennsylvania.

The author is indebted to the secretary of the Royal Anthropologic Institute for permission to quote a short extract from the Proceedings of the Thirtieth International Congress of Americanists, 1952, and to Dr Pott, Director of the Rijksmuseum Voor Volkenkunde, Leiden for permission to reproduce two photographs of the Leyden plate.

Many well-known jades are of necessity omitted, and, since this account was written before Mrs Easby's article on the Squier jades appeared, reference to it is only made in the bibliography.

Fig. 1. One of two opposed low relief figures carved on Stela I at Ixkun. Ornaments believed to be of Jade are in heavy outline.

THE BACKGROUND TO MAYA JADES

The earliest Americans—we believe—crossed into North America over the Behring Straits roughly twenty thousand years ago. They were hunters who spread southward through the continent. Domestication of wild grasses, and the consequent settlement of the wandering hunters produced a number of isolated agricultural communities. The growth of these villages may be said to have begun about 3000 B.C. at the beginning of the pre-classic period. Settlement at La Venta, which was to influence a wide area began about 1500 B.C.; Teotihuacan, the dominant city of Mexico about 300 B.C. There were many others. Perhaps the largest group of homogeneous communities were the Maya who occupied an area from the highlands of Guatemala eastward to the Atlantic coast, and from the valley of the Ulua river in Honduras northward to the Mexican states of Chiapas, Tabasco, and Yucatan in the north. At present we do not know the precise beginnings of Maya civilization nor the cultures which influenced it.

By A.D. 200, which can be regarded as the beginning of the 'classic period', the Maya had evolved a system of hieroglyphic writing. Their astronomical knowledge was considerable and preoccupation with time was probably the real driving force of Maya culture. They were already building ceremonial centres with temples on pyramids, corbelled vaulting and, in the Peten district of Guatemala, they erected stelae to record the passing of time, usually at intervals of twenty years, to correct their calendar and to record the phases of the moon and other astronomical information.

These centres were ruled by a priestly caste whose duties seem to have been entirely concerned with astronomical observations and mathematical calculations. These data were important to them, as they believed that days and longer periods were presided over by different gods, officiating on a rotational system; the fortunes of every day would vary from good to bad according to the character of the presiding gods.

Like their neighbours they were, during the classic period, a

M.J.–B

peasant population ruled by a theocratic oligarchy who built ritual
centres of courts, plazas, pyramids, and temples for the glory of their
gods, and for the pursuit of their astronomical studies. Here the
peasantry assembled to watch the ceremonies, perhaps to make their
sacrifices, and to honour their gods. And the priests in return blessed
their fields and performed the ceremonies to bring rain and fertility.

The economic basis of the culture was the growing of maize by
the *milpa* system of cultivation. Trees were felled in the forest and
burned. Maize seeds were mixed with the ashes in the clearings.
When the soil was exhausted fresh clearings were made. The
common people lived in thatched huts similar to those of the sur-
viving Maya Indians of today. We know that there was extensive
trade all over central America. Pottery from Teotihuacan has been
found at Kaminaljuyu, and one of the best-known jades of Maya
manufacture was found at Teotihuacan. Similarly sculpture on an
early pyramid at Uaxactun in the Peten bears a striking resemblance
to the art of La Venta. While the various classic period civilizations
in Meso-America had the same basic cultural pattern, they differed
immensely in emphasis. It was the Maya calendar which enriched
their religion and stimulated their arts to achievements higher than
those of any other American people.

Between A.D. 900 and A.D. 1000 there seems to have been a dis-
ruption of the Maya civilization of the classic period. No new con-
struction was undertaken and stelae ceased to be erected. Indeed,
the centres may by then have been abandoned.

It was only in Yucatan where Toltec invaders from Tula mingled
with the Maya that a mixed civilization survived, with many characteristics of Maya origin, until it was overthrown by the Spaniards.

The Maya were in essence a stone age people. In their later years
they worked a little gold but could never be described as metal
workers. Their most precious possessions were jade and the green
feathers of the Quetzal bird.

Green, the colour of water—the life-giving fluid—green, the
colour of the maize crop, had special significance to the people of
Meso-America, and both jade and the feathers of the Quetzal bird
were green.

Frequently a small piece of jade was placed in the mouth of the dead. This may have been looked upon as a passport to heaven, but it is more likely that the jade was regarded as having life-giving properties, the spirit or essence of which would be absorbed by the spirit of the deceased and ensure his continued spiritual survival. It is analogous to the Maya practice of burying pottery with the dead and ceremonially killing the vessel by punching a hole in it.

An extreme example of the use of jade as a life preserver may perhaps be seen in the wonderful jade mask found in the tomb under the Temple of the Inscriptions at Palenque and now in the Museo Nacional in Mexico City. This mask is a unique specimen made of a mosaic of small pieces of jade. The burial itself is obviously that of a very great, and probably divine, chief. The mask, covering the whole face with life-giving jade, is doubtless an elaboration of the practice of placing a piece of jade in the mouth.

Jade was important as an object of sacrifice. At Chichen Itza in Yucatan there is a sacred cenote or well, a large hole where the limestone crust of the earth has collapsed, leaving the water beneath open to the sky. This was a place of pilgrimage and sacrifice. On occasions human victims were thrown into the cenote as an offering to the gods, and to convey prayers for rain to them. Should a victim survive until sunset, he was deemed to have been rejected by the gods and pulled out. Pilgrims from far and wide came to cast their offerings into the cenote and when dredging operations were undertaken at Chichen Itza, quantities of jade from all periods and gold from the post-classic period were recovered from it.

This delight in jade was universal in Mesoamerica, and magnificent vases and figurines were made by people belonging to various cultures.

But among the Maya, jade figures were rare. On the other hand beads, plaques, and pendants formed a substantial part of the ritual regalia of priests and rulers. We can form a fair picture of such ornaments from a glance at any of the figures carved on stelae erected throughout the Maya era during the classic period. The drawing of a figure from stela 1 at Ixkun (fig. 1), shows most of the types of Maya jade ornaments. It should be noted, however, that while there are, in archaeological collections in this country and America, examples in jade of all the objects indicated as being made of that material, shell and bone were also used for the same purposes, and no doubt part of the regalia of all but the most important personages may well have been made of these less precious materials.

The conventions of Maya sculpture, too, tended to exaggerate the size and complexity of these ornaments. Priests and rulers wore an elaborate headdress frequently of green quetzal feathers, or sometimes of an animal skin, and possibly embellished with beads for small masks. Ear and nose ornaments were made of jade (see fig. 3). They also wore a necklace of jade beads. This might be a single string supporting a pendant or mask on the breast, or it might be a wide collar with many rows strung together and incorporating plaques of carved jade. Round the waist they had a loin cloth, the elaborately ornamented ends of which hung down like a sporran. Attached to the cloth were elaborate arrangements of beads and feathers. Sometimes a small mask was worn in front of the belt. Occasionally masks were attached over the hips. Wristlets and anklets were also worn. The former often made of tubular and spherical beads. The anklets seem to have been made of hide or skin but the sculptures suggest that in some cases these too were embellished with jade beads.

At Palenque are to be found the remains of some extremely graceful stucco panels where the figures are depicted wearing a skirtlike ornament of a widely meshed beadwork net. These are not unlike a Tibetan devil dancer's apron, but where the Tibetan devil dancer's garment is made of human bone, the Maya figures from Palenque are almost certainly wearing skirts made from tubular jade beads three or four inches long, with spherical beads at their intersection. We know from Aztec mythology that the goddess Chalchiuhtlicue, 'she of the skirt of jade', was so adorned. She was the wife of Tlaloc, the Mexican rain god. While the figure at Palenque is a man, and possibly represents a priest, his skirt is no doubt made of jade beads. (plate I).

THE DATING OF JADE ORNAMENTS

Large quantities of jade were needed for the ritual garments of priests and princes and its scarcity made it the more precious. Pieces of jade would be preserved as heirlooms from generation to generation and would travel far from their place of origin. Jades found in a single tomb would not, therefore, be any guarantee either of contemporaneity or of local origin. Thus dating of individual pieces is very difficult and the normal method of archaeologists of dating by association or stratification does not apply. All that we can say is that no jade will be later than the date of the tomb which we can determine from stratification and the style of the more or less contemporary artefacts. The so-called Leyden plate, however, a simple oval piece of flat jade (plate II), polished and incised on both sides, has on one side an initial series date which reads 'eight Baktuns, fourteen Katuns, three tuns, one uinal,' and twelve days, this corresponds to a date in the year A.D. 320. The other side has a very clearly incised drawing of a priest such as we find on the carved stelae, wearing similar jade ornaments, and with his arms crooked to carry a mysterious object known to archaeologists as a ceremonial bar. The artist had not learned the technique of full representation in profile, and consequently he has shown head and legs facing left, with the torso as viewed from the front, a phenomenon also found on early stelae at Tikal. Until the recent discovery at Tikal of stela 29, this jade held a unique position in Maya archaeology, not only by reason of the incised figure, but because it had the earliest known inscription. It is generally regarded as a convenient marker for the beginning of the classic period. Although this jade was inscribed with a date corresponding to A.D. 320, and therefore one of the earliest inscriptions from the Maya era, it was found near Puerto Barrios in south-eastern Guatemala, in company with a copper bell which could only have been made in the post-classic period, i.e. after about A.D. 1000.

The problem of accurate dating is further complicated by the large number of good forgeries of Mexican jades of all kinds. By far the most common objects found are irregularly spherical beads of various sizes which do not change with time. And often a bewildering variety of styles is found in one hoard as for example in Zacualpa, in the Guatemalan Highlands, difficult to date because of our limited knowledge of stylistic sequence.

Despite these difficulties, a rough and rudimentary chronological classification has been suggested by Kidder and Smith from the

rich finds at Nebaj from which it has been possible to work out a
sequence for flat carved plaques. This is largely in agreement with a
study, made purely from a technological and stylistic point of view
in the British Museum. Even so all dating remains vague and liable
to change in the light of future discoveries.

SOURCES OF JADE

A number of sources of jade are known, notably one at Manzanel. A
large lump weighing some two hundred pounds, from which fragments have been detached to make jewellery, was found in Kaminaljuyu. Much of the raw material came from river beds. The
unworked backs of many pieces show signs of water action, and
many of the irregular subspherical beads have all the appearance of
being water-worn pebbles which have been polished and drilled to
take a thread.

It is quite certain, however, because of the great variety of the
jade, due to differences in the chemical composition of the stones
that they came from many different sources.

Many specimens from Copan, the Peten, and British Honduras
are a brilliant emerald green mottled with white or grey. Some pieces
from Kaminaljuyu are of a bright apple green, and from the Quiché
area further west there is a creamy grey material or sometimes a dull
almost olive green which does not take a very high polish. Olmec
jades from La Venta are of a wonderful bluish colour and specimens
made from this material have been found in some Maya sites. A
lighter blue is found in Costa Rica to the south, and a dull greyish
colour from Teotihuacan in the north.

METHODS OF WORKING

American jade, or more properly jadeite, which is a sodium-alumin-
ium silicate, must be distinguished from the nephrite of New Zealand, which is a calcium-magnesium silicate. But both materials are
extremely hard and tough and difficult to work. While the Maya have
acquired small quantities of gold and copper at the end of the classic
period, they were really a stone-age people and they had to work this
intractable material by stone-age techniques.

Sawing was done by using sand or some similar material as a cutting agent. Two methods were in use. A piece of string, coated with sand, was drawn forward and backward over the piece of jade. After cutting about half way, the jade was turned and a similar cut was made on the other side; when the tang was very thin, the jade was probably tapped with a hammer, leaving a characteristic lenticular fracture scar. Alternatively, a thin flat piece of wood, or possibly slate, was used instead of string, and when the grooves were sufficiently deep, the final detachment was made by a blow of a hammer. It is likely that the latter method was used by the Maya because, so far as the author is aware, no examples of lenticular detachment scars have been found. Again, incised lines could be scratched with a piece of obsidian and once a groove had been formed it could be widened by rubbing sand in it with a finely pointed stick.

The second method of starting a groove, specially suitable for curved lines, was to drill a sequence of shallow depressions almost overlapping, and to rub down the ridges between them. No identifiable remains of a lapidary's workshop have been found, and wooden drills would all have perished by now but the drill bits must almost certainly have been of wood. These were armed with sand or powdered obsidian which provided a keen abrasive edge. As the cutting powder worked free from the end of the drill and spread round the side of the bit, it tended to widen the diameter of the hole, producing a conical depression. Drilling was undertaken from both sides of an object, making the characteristic 'hour-glass' depression, so common in primitive drilling, not only in the Americas but in New Zealand as well.

A more advanced drill, certainly used in the late classic period, and probably before, was the tubular drill consisting either of a hollow reed or else of bird bone. This was armed in the same way with an abrasive powder, and its action was to cut a circular trench leaving a cylindrical core. Such a core was often used as a cylindrical bead.

Very long beads were bored from both ends with the holes meeting in the middle. One flat plaque in the British Museum has a hole about three inches long but only about one-sixteenth of an inch at the narrowest point near the middle. The drill bit must have been a very narrow shaft not less than one and a half inches long. This raises the problem of imparting the necessary rotary motion to the drill point. We know from several manuscripts that fire was made by twirling a stick between the palms of the hands, but the lateral stresses of this method of imparting a rotary motion to the shaft would have broken the point. The same is true of a bow drill used by the Eskimos, though it may well have been used for making large holes. The most likely assumption is that the Maya used a pump-drill. In its most primitive form this mechanism consists of a drill shaft, the top of which is attached to the ends of a cross-bar by two pieces of string (see fig. 2). Before starting work, the drill shaft is rotated in relation to the cross-bar, the string being wound round the drill shaft drawing the cross-bar to the top. The cross-bar is now depressed by the fingers and a rotary motion is imparted to the shaft.

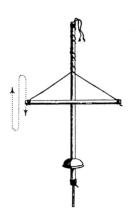

Fig. 2. Pump-drill of the type believed to have been used by the Maya for drilling long holes of small diameter.

Most parts of the pump-drill are made of perishable material, wood and string, but throughout Meso-America numbers of pottery spindle whirls have been found. It has generally been assumed that they were used for spinning cotton but they would make excellent flywheels for pump-drills, and it is reasonable to assume that they were also used on pump-drills for lapidary work.

The high polish of many specimens may have been achieved by rubbing or burnishing with haematite, or more probably with powdered fragments of the stone itself which will wear down the rough surfaces without leaving deep scratches.

It is with such simple tools that the Maya craftsmen produced their masterpieces.

BEADS

The greater part of the regalia of a Maya priest were beads, usually of jade, strung together to form necklaces, or as ornaments on wristlets, anklets, or loin cloths. Most frequently they were roughly spherical water-worn pebbles, drilled with a biconical hole and with a minimum of shaping but highly polished. Occasionally more elaborate beads have been found generally with a series of cusps, three or four being most frequent. One very remarkable bead carved to resemble a Turk's head-knot was found by the British Museum expedition to British Honduras at Pusilha in 1930.

Tubular beads of varying lengths have been found at a number of sites. One kind tapering slightly towards each end and about three inches long is represented in the British Museum's collection by a small group from Pomona. These may very well have been worn as wristlets. Others of a larger diameter were probably the cores obtained in the manufacture of ear flares. The two longest beads in the British Museum, 8¾ inches and 7⅜ inches long respectively were found together at Copan, and almost certainly formed part of an ear ornament assembly. The drilling, even by the expedient of working from both ends, must have been a technical achievement of a high order.

Decoration of tubular beads was rare to judge by archaeological finds, but occasionally specimens with spiral grooving have been found as well as one bead carved in the form of a human figure which is a master piece of jade carving (plate III).

EAR ORNAMENTS

Perhaps the most noticeable single items of jade work depicted in the sculpture and codices are ear ornaments. Children had the lobes of their ears pierced at about the age of 12 years, and through the distended lobe they wore enormous ornaments. The foundation upon which a most complicated structure developed was a trumpet-like ring, generally known as a flare, not usually greater than four inches in outside diameter, and curving inwards to a throat of from one to one and a half inches. These flares were not always, however, worn in the ear. The drawing of the figure on the Leyden plate suggests that the panoply of the figure included two jade flares on his belt, and one on each wrist. Similarly a carving at the Loltun cave shows two flares worn on the belt, and the Maize God (plate IV) from Copan wears, in addition to the two in the normal position, a third over the forehead. There are two very heavy and coarsely made flares which could not possibly have been supported by the lobes of the ear and which may well have been belt ornaments. When these were used as ear ornaments, a neck and backing plate which served to keep the ornament in the lobe of the ear were attached, and these backing plates, by resting against the neck, thrust the flare into a forward facing position. The front of the flare was embellished in various ways.

Quite often a circular disc, known as a throat plate of jade or shell, possibly inlaid, nestled in the opening of the flare. Some of the sculptures on the stelae show a long tassel hanging down from the centre (fig. 3b).

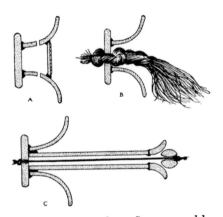

In an even more elaborate form, a long tubular bead emerges from the mouth of the flare to terminate in a miniature flare or a jade bead. A pair of jade miniature fluted flares from Pomona in British Honduras (plate V) probably belong to this type of ear ornament assembly. The arrangement with a small throat plate was probably the earliest. It is not only simple, but is the form depicted in the earlier sculpture. In the late classic period, the tubular bead type of ear ornament is very frequently represented, though at Copan the throat plate type is still found. The tassel form of assembly seems to be late.

Fig. 3. Types of ear flare assembly.

The most usual type of flare curved gently and gradually into the throat, like the mouth of a trumpet, but a variant is known to have been used at Copan and at Kaminaljuyu. In this type, the face of the flare presents a wide flat surface, which turns rather sharply into the throat, the sides of which are at right-angles to it. Examples of this type do not have the same finish. The edge is not always round, but follows the outline of the stone from which they have been cut.

Square flares are very rare, one pair is represented on stela 5, at

Copan, of late classic date, and a single example is in the British Museum's collections, unfortunately from an unknown site in the Highlands of Guatemala. The face of the pair on stela 5 is represented as having diagonally incised lines, and the British Museum specimen, which is quite small (only about two and a half inches across the diagonal) is ornamented by four drilled holes and circles, joined by engraved parallel lines. The whole of the workmanship has that softness of outline which is associated with early jades. Perhaps the most remarkable ear flare ever discovered is a single one of mottled greyish-green jade found at Pomona in the Stann Creek area of British Honduras. It is seven inches in diameter, and the rim slopes gently inwards to curve into the throat which has a diameter of three inches. Its size and workmanship alone would make it the most remarkable jade ever found in British Honduras. The presence of eight glyph blocks arranged in pairs on the face of the flare make it unique. The glyphs are executed in an almost archaic style closely resembling those on the Leyden Plate, which suggests that it must be of a very early date (plate VI).

Partly no doubt owing to the archaic form of the glyphs, and partly because of the difficulty of knowing where to start, and indeed in what order to read the glyphs, the inscription has so far defied interpretation. We can be reasonably certain that it is astronomical or calendrical.

Despite the beautiful workmanship, the scars of the sawcuts made when detaching surplus stone from the back can still be seen, and from these scars it is possible to see how the flare was made. By combining this information with data already published by Kidder, Jennings, and Shook it has been possible to construct a model to show how the various pieces were cut away when making ear flares. Generally, pairs of ear flares were made from a single almost spherical water worn pebble. How this was treated can best be understood by reference to figure 4, which shows how one cylindrical piece suitable for a bead eight large fragments and eight small fragments were detached. The Maya did not waste jade, and the larger offcuts, shaped rather like a sector of an orange, were used to make minor pendants. The other odd fragments were used for inlay or drilled for use as beads.

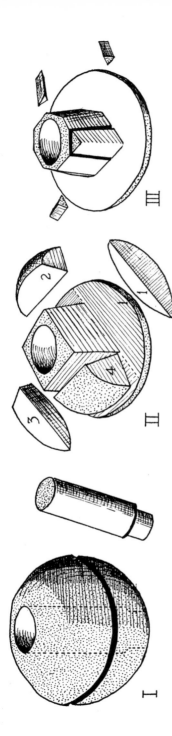
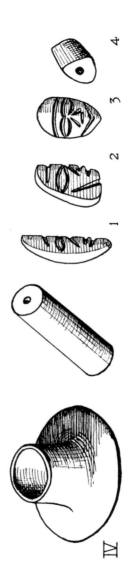

Fig. 4. Stages in the making of ear flares and *the use of the offcuts*. 1. A roughly rounded pebble is drilled from both sides with a tubular drill, and the pebble is then sawn in half. 2. Each half is then cut to detach pieces 1–4, leaving a flange and a roughly square central block. 3. Four small triangular pieces are detached from the central square to produce an octagon. 4. All rough angles are smoothed down by rubbing with abrasives. The offcuts Nos. 1–3 can be used to make miniature pendants similar to those in plate IX; and No. 4, and the cylindrical core to make beads.

No counterpart to the Pomona flare has been found, and it may be that it was intended to be worn in a headdress, on the breast, or in the belt.

INLAY

The use of small fragments of jade to embellish shell ornaments is a rare phenomenon. It is however known from a pair of ear ornaments found at Caracol in British Honduras. They consist of dished circular shells, about three inches in diameter, with an engraved design on the inside. A number of pieces of jade fit exactly into depressions cut in the design and in the centre of each is a large pearl. An engraved shell pectoral ornament from Pomona, and now in the British Museum (plate VII) is further evidence of the use of jade in this way, although the jade is missing, and the shell is much eroded. Circular depressions over the ears of the two opposed figures, where ear flares should be, were intended for a jade inlay.

NOSE ORNAMENTS

Nose ornaments are rarely found in Maya sculpture. Proskouriakoff mentions only about a dozen examples, and these occur in the last part of the classic period. The practice of piercing the septum of the nose came almost certainly from the Highlands of Mexico, but single tubular beads were sometimes worn through the nose, usually with a feather inserted in the hole drilled in the end. Two unbored spindles in the British Museum from an unknown site and certain penannular jades may have been used in this manner.

MINOR PENDANTS AND AMULETS

Excavations at Zacualpa in the Quiché country west of Guatemala City brought to light a number of irregular shaped amulets or pendants so far removed from the carefully worked jades worn as ritual objects that we are tempted to wonder whether they really belong to the Maya at all, or if they do, whether they are not survivals of a long forgotten past, kept for their value as jade. Others in the British Museum, recorded as coming 'from Guatemala' are strictly comparable to them. They are rough irregular pebbles of jade which have been embellished by saw-cuts to indicate limbs and features, occasionally two holes have been drilled to represent eyes. Two or

three have a human form. A very small one with two holes drilled
to represent eyes and a single saw cut for a mouth (plate IX, g) is un-
mistakably a monkey's head. Another irregular pebble, embellished
with a number of saw cuts for limbs, three holes for eyes and mouth
and a little grinding to improve its shape represents a crouching
monkey. Monkeys are a very common motive throughout Meso-
America. They appear in hieroglyphic writing and on the polychrome
pottery of the Maya, and among the Aztecs are frequently found on
pottery stamps used for marking designs in paint on the body. The
symbolism of the monkey varied according to its context, sometimes
meaning the sun, and sometimes representing sexual licence.

Other irregular fragments suggesting a bird's or some animal's
head have been similarly embellished. The bird's head also occurs
frequently in the inscriptions. Birds are often associated with the
world directions, north, south, east, and west, and in head-variants
for the Katuns (twenty year periods).

By far the greater number of these pendants were, however,
human heads or human figures (plate VIII, a–e). A head crudely carved
with saw cuts, but with the eye more elaborately cut out by drilling
and abrasion was found with late classic material at Orange Walk
when the road from Belize to Corozal was being made (plate VIII, b).

Another type (plate IX, a–e) seems to be more formal and to take
on an almost standard form. The back is unworked, save for a hole
drilled for suspension. The front, which forms the face, consists of
two flat vertical surfaces meeting in the middle at an angle of from
forty to one hundred degrees. Often the top of the head is flat,
sometimes both top and bottom. On each of the two flat surfaces are
two almond shaped cuts to represent the eyes. Two oblique saw cuts
and one horizontal one are made for the nose, and another for the
mouth. Above the forehead there may be one or two more saw cuts
to represent either hair or a head dress.

The peculiar shape, not unlike the section of an orange, gives the
clue to the origin of this class of object. In discussing the manufacture of ear flares, we saw how four offcuts of exactly this shape
were removed when shaping the concave lower surface of each flare.
Here then is another proof of the value attached to jade. The offcuts
were not wasted, but used to make pendants.

These crude sketchily made amulets, therefore, were contemporary with the beautifully worked ear flares and the elaborate and beautifully carved regalia of the priesthood. A likely explanation of their purpose is that the crude carvings were intended for use by the poorer agricultural population as amulets. They might almost be likened to the cheap artificial jewellery of our own times.

The same explanation may well be true of the pendants from Orange Walk, which are equally remote in style from the high art of the Maya. But their technique suggests a very early date.

FLAT PENDANTS WITH HUMAN FACES OR FIGURES

There is another, and more elaborate form of pendant, which seems to develop into a conventionalized inconographic formula which can be traced through various technical advances from the early classic to the late classic period. What little archaeological evidence there is tends to confirm the sequence. These are small flat plaques, often not more than about two inches long engraved or carved to represent a human face or figure.

They may have been incorporated in the enormous jade beadwork collars, almost amounting in some cases to capes, depicted on the sculpture. They may also have been incorporated in the headdresses, possibly at the roots of green Quetzal tail feathers like the miniature gold ornaments on the Aztec feather head dress which is preserved in Vienna. More often probably they were worn as single pendants or amulets on a string of beads by less important persons.

The earliest examples were too stylized, and lacking in iconographical detail to identify them with any particular deity.

Their most noticeable characteristics are overall flatness, a lack of emphasis of any particular feature, and shallow grooves delineating the design. The uncut areas are all about the same in size and value. The grooves are fairly wide, and rounded at the bottom. The edges, too, of the grooves are gently smoothed into the surrounding material. The nose is like an inverted T, the alae being indicated by the cross of the T. The sides of the stem turn outward at right angles to form brow-ridges, and the eyes are represented by small rectangular pieces of jade, as also is the mouth. An extreme form of

this kind of face is absolutely rectangular (plate X, a). Unfortunately
we have no record of the provenance of this specimen beyond the
fact that it came from Guatemala. Similar specimens were found at
Nebaj, and at Zacualpa. Others from Chichecastenango are in the
Peabody Museum at Harvard, though none of these display the
same extreme rectangular qualities that the British Museum specimen has. They are, however, clearly of the same type, and one of the
specimens from Chichecastenango, a later variant, shows the use of a
tubular drill to cut lines indicating eyes, mouth, and ear flares. There
are three flares indicated on it. One, in each ear, and one in the
middle of the forehead. Above the flare on the forehead are arcs sweep-
ing down to the ear flares to indicate hair, and above this, are a circular
ornament, probably a glyph, and a spiral scroll possibly representing
maize. This peculiar combination of iconographical elements was to
persist in many carvings of jade, both of faces only, and of full figures.

The earliest example, technologically speaking of a jade of this
kind in the British Museum is illustrated in plate X, e. The composition with three flares is the same but the ornament above the forehead flare is missing. Below the chin, and filling the space between
the ear flares is a string of large beads. The two scrolls above the ear
flares are absent. The features are indicated in the early manner
described above and the carving has some of the soft quality of the
early rectilinear jades without a trace of tubular drilling. It is
however thicker and wider than the rectilinear ones.

At some period a tubular drill was used to cut patterns on jade
and the incidence of this technique is a convenient division between
early and late work.

Other jades with the same formula, even down to the placing of
the scrolls above the ear flares but treated more cursively, are probably of later origin. A series of these types illustrated in plates XI
and XIV, shows the variations. The full figure carvings, both show
a squatting or seated figure, but the composition is the same. The
figure on the flat plaque (plate XI) carries a glyph instead of the forehead flare. No tubular drilling is used, and this jade must belong
to a fairly early period. The other figure, collected in Salvador,
formerly in the collection of the famous French Americanist
Brasseur de Bourbourg, shows a mastery of carving which could

only date it as late classic, though certain details of line suggest a rather remote provincial craftsman (plate XIV, c.)

The pendant (plate XIV, e) shows an elaborately carved example of the face pendant said to have come from Oaxaca, but clearly related to the other Maya jades illustrated. If it does come from Oaxaca, it must have been made in the Maya area, and carried there by trade. Although other writers have regarded this type of jade as being of Zapotec origin, the evidence is against it. One of the best of these pendants is a head from Palenque, given to the Museum by Dr A. P. Maudslay. It is on a larger scale than most of those discussed and is in almost full relief. Other examples occur as subsidiary elements in undoubtedly late classic period plaques from Nebaj and other sites.

We are tempted to ask who is this person so often depicted. There are some grounds for believing that it is the maize god. A small plaque of this type is illustrated in plate XIV, b. It shows a human face with characteristic Maya eyes glancing downward. The nose is indicated by two incised lines carried high above the orbits, and curved to form the eyebrows. Across the forehead, and descending on each side of the face, are a number of arcs, made with a tubular drill, which suggest short curly hair. The figure wears ear flares well represented by drilled circles and a similar ornament over the centre of the forehead. Above the head is a crossed-band glyph generally believed to be a sky sign, flanked by two scrolls representing maize. If we compare this jade with the Maize god from Copan (plate IV) now in the British Museum, we notice the same general expression, and the same close-cropped hair, combined with the same arrangement of three ear flares. On the strength of these features alone we can argue that both the jade and the bust of the Maize god represent the same person. But if we continue the comparison we see that the bust wears a pendant representing a skull with three pendants hanging from it. Comparison with the Maize god in the American Museum of Natural History shows us that these are really bones. Now the only ornaments which are not common to both the jade pendant and to the bust of the Maize god are the crossed band glyph on the pendant, and the skull pendant on the bust. The crossed band glyph is generally regarded as a sky sign. It occurs, among other places, on the celestial bands, and on the sky

monster deluging the Earth in the Dresden Codex, and on the
ceremonial bar carried by the carved figures on many stelae. It
formed, however, the central part of the glyph for completion, and
may well represent the middle portion of the crossed bones sometimes seen on that glyph. The same symbol is also associated with
the god of sudden death. (God E in the Dresden Codex.) The bust of
the Maize god carries an associate with death in the form of the skull
on his breast. This is exactly equated with the crossed band above his
forehead. Thus all the iconographic details of the Maize god bust are
present in the pendant. The youthful Maize god so beloved of the Maya
may well carry the signs of death to symbolize the idea of the cutting
of the maize, and of rejuvenation with the young seed. The idea is the
same as that found in the worship of Attis and Adonis in the old world.

EARLY PENDANTS FROM COPAN

A very unusual group of nine thick pebbles, incised, and ground
into low relief were found in a cache in a mound behind stela 7 at
Copan. They vary both in subject matter and in style of working.
But all are either carved in very low relief with rounded contours
or have the features indicated by rather broad incised lines, and in
one, an ear flare is clearly made by incising and not with a tubular
drill. These features point to an early, and possibly pre-classic date.
The low relief with little emphasis, and the shallow incised lines
are similar to earlier forms of flat plaques, or pendants and have
none of the qualities of jades which on stylistic grounds must belong
to the late classic period.

One, a small head with a simple head dress (plate XII, d) has the
features indicated by very low relief. Another (plate XII, a) shows a
kneeling figure, with a large head more like the traditional nursery
representation of Humpty Dumpty. Two showing monsters with
human heads in their mouths, and one, a face framed by the upper
and lower jaw of the same class of monster probably representing
the sun at sunset when it was believed to enter the jaws of an
enormous mythical creature, whose whole upper jaw was the sky,
and whose lower jaw was the earth. Two more representing hunch-
backs are smooth and rather indefinite in their features. The form
probably being suggested by the shape of the pebbles, which were

slightly modified. In another pair, arms and legs appear in curiously contorted positions; in one immediately above the head, and in another, one leg and one arm appear immediately behind it (plate XIII). They possibly represent jugglers or acrobats. We know that among the Aztecs, dwarfs and jugglers had a position not far removed from that of a court jester in Medieval Europe, but it was their fate to be sacrificed on occasions of eclipses of the sun. If our interpretation is correct, these two jades are a remarkable attempt to break away from the conventional representation of all of the human body, and to show the subject as a visual impression.

Taking the group as a whole, the only features common to all are the matching pale green colour, and the suggestion of antiquity. Differences in style and workmanship, although they all indicate an early date suggest that they were made by different workmen, probably at different times, and possibly even at different places, yet the almost perfectly matching colour leads us to believe that they are carefully collected for a particular offering, the precise purpose of which will almost inevitably remain a mystery.

NATURALISTIC PENDANTS IN THE ROUND

Pendants of this kind are very rare and date from the late classic period. A beautifully carved head from the cenote of sacrifice at Chichen Itza is perhaps unique among this class of object in bearing a date corresponding to A.D. 648.

The British Museum has two specimens. The first excavated at Pusilha measures only 1¼ inches in height and was probably made at about the same time. It shows a typical Maya head, with prominent nose, and slightly receding chin. The right eye is naturalistic but the left is a minute detachable plug, now loose, but probably fixed with some adhesive long since perished. Probably the artist found a flaw in the jade after carving the other side, and rather than discard a piece of jade, which he had worked on, devised this ingenous repair.

SOME OUTSTANDING JADES

Every civilization produces some works of art which far excel those by other artists of the same period. The Maya were no exception.

From Copan we have a seated figurine of greyish green jade (cover), $7\frac{1}{4}$ inches high, representing either a god or a priest. He wears on his head a turban-like head dress embellished with a glyph-like jewel, bordered by beads. There are two ear flares, and round his neck is a string of beads which is tied at the back by a knotted string. The backs of the beads remain unworked although the artist had been at great pains to indicate the knot—a suggestion that the gorgeous finery so often depicted in the sculpture was only intended to be seen by the populace from the front. The priest would stand in front of a temple, set high on a pyramid while the people stood and wondered below. He wears on his breast a small plaque or pendant similar to those described above; a loin cloth of some plaited material, with a disc or flare in front, and on the tassel another disc—the Maya sign for jade. It is possible to date this figure. The representation possible of the pupils by two vertical incisions is suggestive of the formative period figurines. The inverted T-shaped nose and the clenched position of the arms, typical of the early stelae, the Leyden Plate, and the flat plaque described above, and illustrated in plate XI, clearly point to the early classic period.

Rather more difficult to date is a long tubular bead, (plate III), drilled from end to end. The position of the forearms suggests a similar early period, but this piece is full of iconographical detail, which modifies the normal features. In the head dress is the sign for completion. The eyes, rectangular with a small subsidiary rectangle in the corners to represent pupils, giving the impression of squinting, are indicative of the face variant for the numeral four, and so of the God of number four—the aged sun god, the husband of the moon goddess, called Akanehob—'he with the squint who cries aloud'—by the modern Lacandon Indians. The crossed bands, associated with the heavens, in the mouth are an unusual substitution for the normal filed teeth associated with this god, but are not inappropriate. They may serve to indicate the sun god high in the heavens at midday, but this is only speculation. The style of the ornaments, is of course influenced by the limited space on the bead, but the rather stiff treatment indicates that this example almost certainly came from Quirigua.

A large jade head (plate XVI) entirely without embellishment is said

to have come from Copan. It is a highly polished naturalistic representation of a young Maya with an artificially flattened forehead. The
eyes are treated in the regular manner of the late classic period.
Perhaps the only weakness is the straight saw cut across the partly
opened mouth, which contrasts sharply with the delicate modelling
of the nose and lips. The back, slightly concave in a vertical plane,
is inscribed all over with glyphs. Provision is made for suspension
by three pairs of conical holes drilled from back and side, one pair
placed at the top, and the others on each side. It weighs three
pounds fourteen ounces, and is seven inches high and almost four
inches wide. Although the specimen is unique as far as specimens in
museums are concerned, and in spite of its weight the occurrence of
similar sized masks worn as breast or waist ornaments on the monu-
mental sculpture leaves little doubt as to its purpose. There is however some doubt as to its provenance. The extreme cranial deforma-
tion and the absence of ornament are not so reminiscent of Copan as
of Palenque whence comes another mask, smaller and made of
stucco, but of very similar style.

A small but very beautiful, almost olive green jade mask, excavated by Eric Thompson at Tzimin Kax (plate XV a) offers many
puzzling features. The simplicity of the composition, the trilobal
coiffeur, and the curious treatment of the eyes—almond shaped
depressions, with the pupils indicated by two small drilled holes
seem to be right outside the normal traditions of Maya art, and this
piece may well have been imported. It is unusual in having a depression hollowed out of the back by tubular drilling—perhaps as a
space for some minute charm or relic. The jade is too small for this
to have been done to lighten it.

Of similar colour is a rectangular ornament drilled for suspension
showing a figure carved in late classic style, slightly angular, and
with curious rectilinear panels on the plain surfaces, presumably
intended to receive glyphs like the lintels from Yaxchilan. The most
interesting feature about this plaque is that the carved surface is in
two planes. When the piece was detached from the parent block the
two sawcuts from opposite sides did not meet exactly, but the artist
was sufficiently skilled to carry his design successfully over the
change in levels.

Far surpassing this in skill, however, is the plaque found at
Teotihuacan (frontispiece). Of irregular shape, but with finely
trimmed edges it is $5\frac{1}{2}$ inches high, and $5\frac{1}{2}$ long at its widest place.
The design seems to have been cut off by the edges. This may
be due to one of two reasons, either it was part of a mosaic design of
a number of similar pieces, or it was part of a larger plaque which
had been broken and subsequently trimmed and adapted for wear
as an ornament. The suspension holes drilled near the top may well
have been later additions.

The design itself consists of a rather corpulent Maya dignitary
sitting cross-legged on a throne, which resembles the sign for the
day Cauac. He is looking to his right, and inclining his shoulder
slightly, to speak to a small figure, either a prisoner or suppliant in
the bottom left-hand corner of the plaque. He wears an elaborate
head dress consisting of part of the head of a monstrous animal,
bedecked with discs of jade or shell, and three tail feathers of the
Quetzal bird. He wears ear flares with beads, a bar-like breast
ornament, wristlets, anklets, a shield with a grotesque face, and a
loin cloth with a mask like those on the pendants believed to represent the Maize god. From his mouth issues a florid scroll probably
representing speech.

At the top of the plaque are two interlaced designs suggesting
mats, the symbol of authority not only among the Maya but among
the Aztecs as well, and on the extreme left is a small figure whose
head bears a close resemblance to the face variant, and therefore to
the god, of number seven.

This remarkably beautiful plaque, among the highest achievements of the Maya lapideries was found at Teotihuacan far from its
original home. A plaque equal to it in quality and generally similar
in style and composition was found at Nebaj in the Alta Vera Paz,
and the famous polychrome vase from the same site also shows a
dignitary in the same posture. Two minor fragments showing
comparable workmanship and style clearly belong to the same
school. These, with plaques of similar workmanship, but differing
in so far as they depict seating figures in full front view, represent
the peak of Maya lapidary's work in jade.

BIBLIOGRAPHICAL NOTE

The general reader who wishes to know more about the Maya and their place in the growth of Ancient American culture, should consult

J. Eric S. Thompson: *The Rise and Fall of Maya Civilization* (London, 1956).

Sylvanus G. Morley: *The Ancient Maya,* Stanford University Press (1946) or subsequent editions.

Pal Keleman: *Medieval American Art* (New York, 1946), illustrating many fine jades.

T. W. F. Gann, *Maya Jades,* Proceedings of the 21st International Congress of Americanists, pp. 274–82 (Göteborg, 1925).

Students are also referred to the Excavation Reports of the Division of Historical Research of the Carnegie Institution of Washington, D.C., and to the Reports of the University Museum of Pennsylvania. Among the Carnegie Institution (referred to below as C.I.W.) reports consulted in the preparation of this work were:

Samuel Kirkland Lothrop: *Zacualpa, a Study of Ancient Quiche Artifacts,* C.I.W. Publication No. 472 (1936).

A. V. Kidder: *The Artifacts of Uaxactuan, Guatemala,* C.I.W. Publications No. 576 (1947).

A. V. Kidder and A. L. Smith: *Excavations at Nebaj, Guatemala,* C.I.W. Publication No. 594 (1951).

A. V. Kidder, J. D. Jennings, and E. M. Shook: *Excavations at Kaminuljuyu, Guatemala,* C.I.W. Publication No. 561 (1946).

John M. Longyear III: *Copan Ceramics,* C.I.W. Publication No. 597 (1952).

Tatiana Proskouriakoff: *Classic Maya Sculpture,* C.I.W. Publication No. 593 (1950).

J. Eric S. Thompson: *Maya Hieroglyphic Writing, Introduction,*
C.I.W. Publication No. 589 (1950).

These deal respectively with the sculpture and with the glyphs
and the mythology associated with them.

Also of great interest is:

Elizabeth K. Easby, The Squier Jades from Tonina, Chiapas,

Essays in Pre-Columbian Art and Archaeology. (Harvard University
Press) 1961.

W. F. Foshag and R. Leslie, *Jadeite from Manzanal, Guatemala.*
American Antiquity 21: 81-83, 1955.

PLATE I. Dancing figure wearing skirt of jade beads; stucco panel
at Palenque.

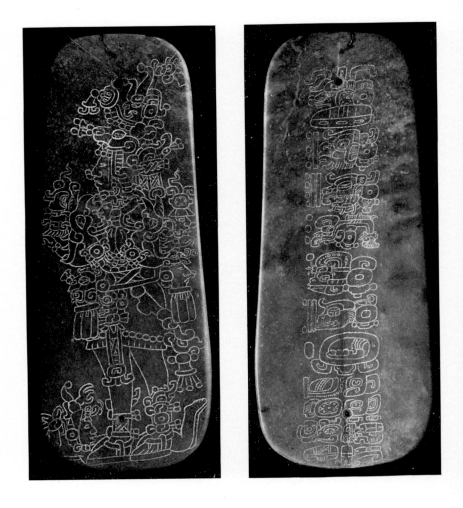

PLATE II. The Leyden Plate: a jade plaque. On one side is incised a figure of a priest, or ruler: on the other, the Maya date 8 Baktuns, 14 Katuns, 3 Tuns, 1 Uinal, and 12 Kins, corresponding to A.D. 320.

PLATE III. Tubular bead, carved in the form of a human figure, possibly representing the sun god, who may be identified by the shape of the eyes, and the crossed bands in the mouth.

PLATE IV. Limestone figure of the Maize God, from Copan, wearing jade flares in each ear, and over the forehead.

PLATE V. Types of ear flare: left-hand side, miniature fluted ear flares from Pomona; right-hand side, flat engraved ear flare of early type, and typical trumpet-like ear flare of the classic period.

PLATE VI. The Pomona flare: with a diameter of seven inches. This is the largest flare discovered. The glyphs have not been interpreted: but the style, similar to that on the Leyden plate, suggests a very early date.

PLATE VII. Carved shell Pectoral from Pomona: the design shows
two kneeling Maya dignitories facing each other; over the ear of
each there is a circular depression intended for an inlay of jade
to represent the ear flare.

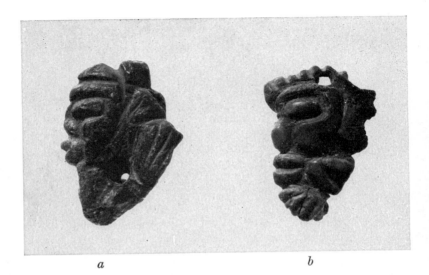

a   b

c   d   e   f

PLATE VIII. Minor pendants: above, profile type made without use
of a drill, right-hand specimen from Orange Walk, British Honduras, probably pre-classic or early classic; below, human figure
type made by embellishing natural pebbles with the minimum of
cutting.

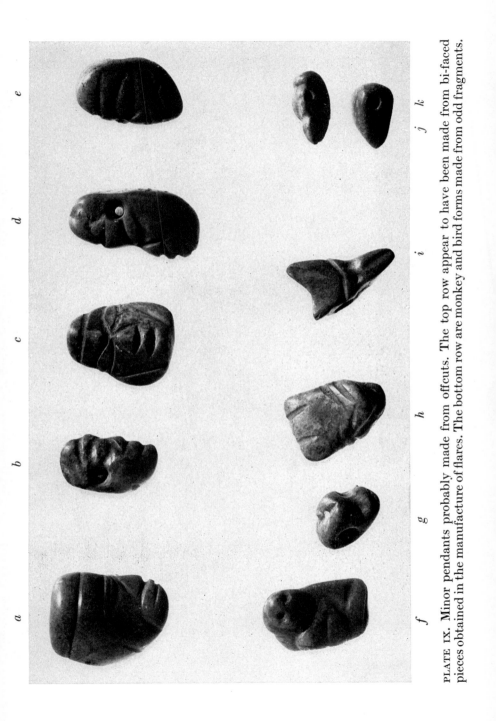

PLATE IX. Minor pendants probably made from offcuts. The top row appear to have been made from bi-faced pieces obtained in the manufacture of flares. The bottom row are monkey and bird forms made from odd fragments.

a   b   c   d   e

f   g   h   i   j   k

PLATE X. Early flat pendants. In this series there is evidence of the use of a tubular drill only in *d*.

PLATE XI. Flat, full figure pendant. An early date is attributed to this piece because the circular ornament shows the irregularities indicating that a tubular drill was not used.

PLATES XII AND XIII. Engraved pebbles of apple-green jade from a substela cache at Copan. Plate XII: *a, d,* faces; *b,* face in mouth of a serpent;

a

b

c

d

c, e, faces in mouth of a monster, possibly representing the sun being
swallowed by the earth monster. Plate XIII: *a, b, c, d*, jugglers.

PLATE XIV. Flat pendants of the late classic period: *a*, from Chichicastenango, *b*, equated with Maize God (see plate IV), *c*, from San Salvador, *d*, from Palenque, *e*, said to come from Oaxaca, but of Maya style